NEW YORK RE
POETS

RON PADGETT is a poet and translator. His book *How Long* was a Pulitzer Prize finalist in poetry in 2012 and his *Collected Poems* won the 2014 Los Angeles Times Book Prize in poetry. He is the recipient of a Frost Medal from the Poetry Society of America for lifetime achievement. Padgett's translations include *Zone: Selected Poems of Guillaume Apollinaire* (NYRB). Seven of his poems were used in Jim Jarmusch's film *Paterson*. New York City has been his home base since 1960.

Ron
Padgett

Pink Dust

NYRB/POETS

 NEW YORK REVIEW BOOKS *New York*

THIS IS A NEW YORK REVIEW BOOK
PUBLISHED BY THE NEW YORK REVIEW OF BOOKS
207 East 32nd Street, New York, NY 10016
www.nyrb.com

Some of these poems appeared in a small book of mine called So Say So
(Scram Press, 2021) and in the magazines Poetry Daily, The Café Review,
and Three Fold. *Thanks to the editors.—R.P.*

Library of Congress Cataloging-in-Publication Data
Names: Padgett, Ron, 1942– author.
Title: Pink dust / by Ron Padgett.
Description: New York: New York Review Books, 2025. | Series: New York
  Review Books Poets |
Identifiers: LCCN 2024039871 (print) | LCCN 2024039872 (ebook) | ISBN
  9781681379081 (paperback) | ISBN 9781681379098 (ebook)
Subjects: LCSH: Aging—Poetry. | LCGFT: Poetry.
Classification: LCC PS3566.A32 P56 2025 (print) | LCC PS3566.A32 (ebook)
LC record available at https://lccn.loc.gov/2024039871
LC ebook record available at https://lccn.loc.gov/2024039872

ISBN 978-1-68137-908-1
Available as an electronic book; ISBN 978-1-68137-909-8

Cover and book design by Emily Singer

Printed in the United States of America on acid-free paper.
10 9 8 7 6 5 4 3 2 1

In memory of Dick Gallup

Every time I approach a blank page
the poems in it shout, "Oh no!
Here he comes again! Run!"
I grab at them as they flee
like terrified little bugs.

Gotcha!

Contents

Residue

There used to be an eraser
in the shape of a wheel, pink,
attached to a little brush, black,
for erasing pencil words
and then brushing away the residue,
a little pink dust,
though I preferred
to brush it away with my hand
or puff up my cheeks
and blow it away.
I'd like to replay
all those moments in my life
one after the other,
in a film to be called
A History of Pink Dust.

Wasn't it the Bible
that said
"Blessèd art thou
among women"?
I'm taking those words
for myself,
as I am blessed—
nay, blessèd
to be in a house
with one of them,
the most beautiful
old woman in the world.
There is nothing
more beautiful
than a beautiful old woman.

In Mexico
at sixteen
I saw a play
in Spanish,
a language I didn't know,
and at one point
a man with a mustache
crashed through a wall
and sat on a chair.
No one paid him
the slightest attention.

Star Joe

Joe said,
"The reason I'm a painter
is because I'm not a movie star."
The reason I'm a poet
is because I'm not a zebra.
I am, though,
for a moment,
caught inside the word *zebra*,
z to a,
and I alternate
from inside this page
to outside it, inside,
out, and so on.
Joe a *movie* star?
He was a star, period.

Grrrr Back

If I didn't have a conscience
I'd go loping around
biting trees and waving my claws
at the night sky,
for I would be a wolf man,
wearing clothes
but doomed to a very sad life.
Instead, I get to wear clothes
and wave my claws at myself.

Imagine editing a book and calling it
An Anthology of French Poets from Nerval to Valéry in
    English Translation.
Such a one appeared in 1958.
Imagine you are a young poet
who bought it a few years later
for $1.45, read it
cover to cover, delighted,
transported, and sometimes bored by it.
Imagine that many years later
a friend tells you
the editor was his uncle!
Imagine that you are the mouse
who nibbled a lacemark
along the edge of the cover.
Imagine that you are the book itself,
standing on a shelf for forty years,
and then someone takes you down,
holds you, opens you,
and falls in love with you again.

And Where It Lands

When I was ten years old
I set up a target in our backyard
and from the front yard I shot
arrows over the roof.
You'd be surprised how quickly
a kid can get good at it.
This was a skill that later served me well
when I faced the challenges
of adult life. It helped me
never to become a dolt.

Cuff Mode

The dark blue cuffs on my shirt
stick way out from under
my gray sweater.
They look cute!
It pleases me
to have a cute *accoutrement*,
as if I were the embodiment
of my old idea of what
it's like to be French.

One Poem or Three Poems

I look down
at my dark green flannel shirt
and watch it console me
as its sleeves cover the arms of my grandfather.

◆ ◆ ◆

It's good to get up
before the faint glow of sunrise,
as if you were going out
to milk the cows
and lead them down to the pasture
that is now filled with pines.

◆ ◆ ◆

When I write a poem
I have a battle with myself,
but when I finish,
it falls silent, the battle,
and moves away
like ancient Greeks
looking for another place to fight.

I wish my mother and father
would have been able to open
a window and look in
to see their own personalities,
and to have found me
sitting in there waiting for them,
so they could have opened
a window in me too,
but it didn't happen,
and we all three stayed
who we didn't think we were.
It's too bad,
we could have known how
wonderful we were!

Seesaw

I'm trying to remember
why I enjoyed playing
on the teeter-totter,
going up and down, up and down
endlessly. I think
I liked only going up,
though if I let myself
come down hard enough to bang
the ground it made the other child
fly up off the seat and scream.

When I was a child
my heroes were grown-ups
and when I grew up
I saw that my heroes
had been children dressed as grown-ups,
and that heroes beyond that
were beings I could not begin
to imagine, as they
looked like ordinary people,
rather uninteresting.

If

"And well it's if if if if if"
sang the green bells of Cardiff.
I didn't know you could climb that ladder
as if up the Château d'If
but once I did
there was no going down.

George Schneeman would not eat a lobster.
"They're too noble," he said,
"it's like eating a prehistoric creature."
That was the real George,
angular in thought
and unapologetic.
If you think he was odd,
I don't want to know you.
Go eat a lobster.

A Few Blocks

Grasping a twisted bedcover with both hands,
with cleavage exposed and one leg poking
out from what
looks like a baggy shirt,
orange, a man's maybe, she
turns her anguished, lustful eyes toward you
on the cover of *Vital Detective Cases*,
with "Murder in the Bedroom" below
and "Lust Monster of Brooklyn" above,
"March 25¢."
This is 1954,
published just a few blocks
from where Edwin Denby was living.
One ad inside is for a book
called *How to Get Along in This World.*
No mention of the one after that.
I guess you have to get murdered
or, like Edwin, murder yourself.

When, from bed,
I *thought* to ask my wife
to turn off the light,
she walked across the room
without my saying a word,
and turned off the light.
What a joy,
this strange new power I have
over her.

Robert Creeley

A few years before his death, Robert Creeley
gave a reading of his poetry
at the Maison de l'Amérique Latine in Paris,
and near the end of it he said
"I'm going to read some new work now,
all of it plain old doggerel."
It was.
As he read he seemed half amused, half embarrassed.
I cringed with a weird delight.
It was the most avant-garde thing
I had seen in a long time.
The people gave each other furtive looks.

◆　◆　◆

Recently I wrote a poem that said
that making scones was a good thing to do.
It could not have been more commonplace.

◆　◆　◆

The first poems I remember reading
came from books like *Best Loved Poems of the American
    People.*
"The gingham dog and the calico cat
side by side on the table sat,"
"But there is no joy in Mudville—mighty Casey has struck
    out,"
and one about the cremation of a man named Sam McGee.
I was around thirteen.

I thought some of them were pretty good.
"And the road was a ribbon of moonlight over the purple
moor."
Terrific! (But what's a moor, exactly?)

◆ ◆ ◆

I see Bob's face
in that moonlight.
He taps with his whip on the shutters.

Against the Grain

Once in a museum I saw the Bible
on a grain of rice
displayed under a microscope.
I saw words but wasn't
going to stand there
and read the entire Bible.
I've never stood *anywhere*
long enough to read the entire Bible.
In fact I've never read the entire Bible.
This morning, though,
I did eat a bowl of rice
with hot milk, sugar, butter, and salt.
That's a lot of Bibles I ate.

When I was around ten
someone said that if
I put some horse hairs
in a jar of water
and left it in full sunlight
the hairs would turn
into snakes, and so
I did, and when
I went back a week later
there was the jar,
full of small snakes,
which I heaved
into the shrubbery
and never said a word
to anybody
it was so horrible.

Uncle James

After seeing combat
in World War II as a sailor
in the Pacific theater
my uncle James returned home ready to eat.
By 1950, still in his twenties,
he had developed a small paunch,
which he found amusing.
After big holiday dinners
he would remove his shirt,
turn sideways, and undulate
his abdomen, wave after wave,
like the ocean, then burst
out laughing as my aunt
chided him, "Oh, *James*,"
incorrigible child that he was.
I liked his undulations and the squint
that wrinkled up his smiling face
as he looked at us for approval
or disapproval, both the same
to him, for he was alive
and eating all he could hold.

Picture Perfect

A male and female duck
glide across the pond, she
leading him in what I assume
is a mating move and then
they glide up into the air.
I take a tissue and blow
as the tenor and soprano
rise side by side on waves
on the radio.
In the next room my wife is
reaching for a tissue of her own,
unaware of being
so perfectly in this picture.

There are few people of conscience
who can read Reverdy
and not feel as if
they have committed the sin
of not being serious enough,
deeply serious, so serious
as to make one drop to the ground
and wonder how to get back up,
as he did, time and again,
only to look in the mirror
and see the face
vanish the moment
he thought to speak to it.
Bedrock. You have it
or you don't.

I sat around until it was dark
and had a cigarette, the same one
I smoked in 1958
in a hotel room in Mexico late at night
with twelve teenage girls smoking
Mexican cigarettes and laughing
into the smoke of each other's breaths.
It was a Delicado,
slightly flattened and with pinstripes
running along its length
that went all the way
to a little Mexican infinity inside me.

Baseball Bat Perdu

It strikes me,
like a one-inch baseball bat
to the head,
that what I do
is a complete waste of time,
but that the best thing I *can* do
is to waste time.
What else can you do with it?

A Brief Guide to Twentieth-Century American Poetry

Pound was a verb,
Eliot a noun.
They sentenced us to modernity.
Williams was a definite article,
Stevens a what?
Stein was a paragraph
and then a paragraph.
Stein a paragraph.
I mean a wall.
Guess what?
I still like them all.

Four Quartets

Curious, everything's
different in the big picture
while in the little picture
it's exactly the same.
I am a window
set to music and played
by the Concertgebouworkest
of Amsterdam.

There are four correct answers
to every question:
a right one, a wrong one,
both of them right, and both wrong.
How funny and lovely the notes
as they float out
to the big little world
out there.

As a young adult
I found my heart beating
in odd rhythms
whenever I drank a cup of coffee,
so I stopped.
In those days
it was almost impossible
to get decaffeinated coffee
in Europe, so it was sad
to be in a café in Paris
or a *bar* in Rome,
though the sadness
had a beauty of its own.
Many decaffeinated years went by,
and I found myself
in Vienna, alone
in the elegant old coffeehouse
of the Hotel Sacher,
and I let go
with a full-bore cup
and a Sacher torte and lit up
like a palace full of sparkling people,
and there was Lenin
over there, and Freud,
and psychoanalysis and history
rising into the air hazy
with the smoke of cognition
and I knew that finally I was in
a world I had been longing for
without even knowing it.

Geezer

As a young man I wanted to live
a long time so I could know
what it feels like to be old.
Now I'm trying to remember
what it feels like to be young.
Young old, old young.
Do you need more proof
of how ridiculous I am?
If so, look inside yourself,
for you are just like me.
There is nothing more ridiculous
than a human being.
The rest of nature doesn't know this.
It's our little secret.

Fuck, you
don't *feel* like you're seventy-seven plus—
I mean in your mind
you come in at around oh,
I don't know, fifty?
I *do* know I almost
still have a sense of humor.
I'll show you:
"A bar walked into a bar..."

What is it that,
in the face of death,
lets you find yourself
sitting in a chair
with happiness all around you
and in you and of you,
as if you were a dog
and your master is petting your head
and telling you how good
you are, forever?

Here is the handwriting of an old man,
wiggly like the hairs on his head
and the even more wiggly ones
in his memory of the eyebrows of his grandfather
who fought in the Civil War
and had his first shave outside a tent, in Georgia
two years before a man with a gray beard
leaned over his field hospital cot and kissed him on the lips
and signed the letter "Your loving son"
in as graceful a script as he could with tears in his eyes.

Now, just how
did I get here—
staggering old gent
in a coat and hat
and another coat, hey,
it's cold outside,
and outside is where
we are, right?
If I told you I'm seventy-eight
you'd say something
I wouldn't like,
so I'll just stand here
and look at you
and *think* of saying seventy-eight.
And you—I didn't
catch your name.
(As if I cared.)

It's something of a relief
to fritter away a few hours
doing not much of anything
other than walking around
and looking at things
that aren't in any way remarkable,
and to know
that, of the diminishing hours
left in your life,
you are frittering some away,
something you can't remember
ever doing before,
relaxing into nothing in particular.

I'm sure I'm
not the only person
my age
who is still asking
the same questions
about existence
that I asked
in adolescence,
but sometimes
when I look at the faces
of people my age
all I see are loaves
of bread, smiling,
as if baking
had been a great pleasure.

I shovel a path
from the porch to the truck
and another around the house
to the back door, stopping
to see if I'm one
of those geezers
who have heart attacks
while shoveling snow,
and when I'm finished
I'm not. Look
at all that snow out there
going down the hill
as far as the eye can see.

Sex can continue
into old age
in various ways,
a fact
that no one wants
to talk about.
But it's interesting!
Much more than the sex of youth,
which has so much force
it can't be interesting,
it's like being hit in the head
with a hammer.
Sex in old age
is more like being
covered with warm snow
by an angel
who pretends to be blushing,
radiant with joy.

You get to a certain age
and you start sitting around
waiting
for the future,
as now there's no reason
to rush toward it
as you did when you didn't think
it existed, not really,
and now, funny thing,
soon enough you'll be right.

In Memory of Dick Gallup

You have a cup of tea
and take a nap for eternity
which, as my very old grandmother said,
with a strange gleam in her eye,
is a *very* long time.
It didn't take long
to drink that cup of tea,
that poor little cup of tea.

I had a friend,
an old Vermonter
who died in the house
he was born in,
at ninety-four, alone.
His name was Harold Clough.
He did manual work
all his life
until he quit working
around the age of eighty-seven.
I just looked at the picture
of him on my wall
and wondered what
he'd think of me now.
I never heard him say
anything good or bad about anyone.
In fact, I never heard him
say *anything* about anyone.
He was always quietly happy.

When I was a sensitive adolescent
pink clouds in a blue sky sent me
into a cylinder of pleasure,
but now that I'm old
I see them and,
as if they were peasants
walking along a country lane,
I simply nod, happy enough
just to see them,
with no cylinder involved.

Forever Enough

I put some stamps
on the envelope, maybe enough,
I don't know.
The post office
should accept it
as is, because
I made an effort.
The post office should look
at the envelope and say,
"Well, he made an effort."

In my sleep I caressed you
and when I woke up
I caressed the memory
of the dream.
I never caressed you
in "real life."
I never even wanted to
though I was close
to liking the idea of caressing you.
If I had caressed you
I would remember it,
which is what I did last night.

Lockdown

If I were living alone
there wouldn't be enough people in the house,
just as a house without doorways
has something missing.
A world without people
would be okay, though.
In fact I think it would be wonderful.
Everything would be a fact.

I have no sense
of who Haydn was
in his personal life,
what the street felt like
as he walked down it
in Vienna in
the eighteenth century,
and how, at home,
his mind opened up
to reveal boxes
on top of boxes
with strings between them
in patterns
where small dots were jumping.
All he had to do
was paint it all
silver, white, and light blue
and hurl his name into it,
Franz Joseph Haydn.

A light-blue silken thread flies up
and forms an arch across the sea
to my head, and along this line
a shimmering voice calls out my name
so sweetly that I want to live,
for who would want to leave
a world with such a thread?

£sd is not LSD,
it's pounds, shillings, and pence.
Put £sd and LSD together
and what have you got?
An unbelievable amount of nothing.

Dare to express your inner self
in the privacy of your own mind
but please don't think
other people want to hear it.
There are too many other inner selves
to keep track of as it is.
Instead, express your *outer* self.
Just stand there.

I guess New York is doing okay
without me, though I don't see how,
since I'm an essential part
of its being there. The part I took away
I have here now,
a big translucent chunk
that every now and then goes *pop*
like a flashbulb suddenly too hot to touch.

I almost feel sorry
for the human thumb,
off to the side, alone,
and not looking much like
its four brothers and sisters—
the real fingers.
They invite the thumb
to help them when they need it,
but otherwise keep their distance.
Just across the way, though,
there's another thumb.
In the old days
the two used to twiddle.
Now they're happy enough
just knowing they're both there.

I noticed a black thing—
a crumb of chocolate cake?
a single mouse dropping?—
and for a moment
I didn't want it to be there
on my desk, so I flicked it off
and onto the floor. Now
it's down *there*.
I wonder what it is.

It's satisfying to eat
exactly the right amount
of, say, French toast
and then stop,
for you have just
achieved a moral victory
in the middle
of the flow of time,
and though it flows away,
this victory,
you have its aftertaste,
along with butter
and genuine Vermont maple syrup
from a tree not far down the road.

Jesus would have made things
a lot easier if he had written
his memoirs, but he was too busy
being Jesus, I suppose.
That's pretty much all I have
to say about him right now.
He's like mercury: You touch it
and it slips away, then stops
and waits for you to try again.
He's too hide-and-seek for me.
That cave, for instance.

Sometimes I surprise myself
by liking myself
when I laugh at myself
as if at someone else,
someone I like.
When I stop laughing
I look around
like a guy who wakes up
and has no idea where he is,
with the Eiffel Tower
right outside the window,
and he laughs, in French.

Was it in the film *Stalag 17*
that one of the prisoners
flexed his index finger
repeatedly
while chanting
"*Ex*-er-cises, *ex*-er-cises,
we must do our *ex*-er-cises"?
I'm supposed to be doing
my exercises right now,
but I'm suddenly melancholic
at the thought of that guy's finger.

What's left?
One more dead mouse?
Or a peony
in a soft white marble hand,
it's pink, that flower—
as if a Canova,
a genius, that sculptor.
Beautiful things come to me
on their own and I,
an old man,
feel them wash over me,
except for the mouse.
Him I throw out in the bushes.

See that robin over there
by the house?
Why is he just standing there?
Shouldn't he be hopping
or looking around?
He's the first robin
of the year.
So let him just stand there!
And now he's gone,
perhaps in search
of a better poet.

I just did twenty-five push-ups,
vacuumed the floor,
then dropped down
and did twenty more,
for what reason I cannot say
or even want to think about,
especially at this moment
when I'm still breathing hard.

I almost didn't know what
day it is and then
I did, clicked into time,
suddenly more secure
that it's Thursday!
Which means nothing
or next to nothing.
I am next to nothing.
It's in this room with me,
an old pal.

Snow falling from gray sky,
it's time to bake,
scones, I mean,
and right out of the oven
take one and butter it,
with jam, teapot hot at hand,
and exult in the face
of everything horrible.

My ancestors were wee Celtic folk,
about thirteen inches tall
was the average, so
they made little tiny watches
out of stone, stone watches
they were, hundreds of them,
and then rolled them
down a hill all at once.
Down, down they went.

I repeat the words
John Wayne said
in the film *Rio Bravo*:
"Burdette! Burdette! Nathan Burdette!"
But Nathan Burdette
doesn't want to come out
and face John Wayne.
So John Wayne stands there
saying, "Burdette! Burdette! Nathan Burdette!"

A haiku went up into a tree
and sat there on a limb
it had just made up.

I thought 2020
was going to be a great year,
like perfect eyesight.
Look out the window and *fwoop*
2020 disappears
into a robin redbreast.

Air
light
energy
and love
all so great
to have just above.
Anytime you reach up
you can grab one
or what the heck
all of them
and hurl them
around the room
like colors
that make you happy.

When I sang "Old Riley"
he fell out
of the bomb-bay doors
of his B-29
on a bombing run
over Germany, 1944,
calling back to me,
"Where did you learn that song?"

Baking is a lovely thing to do,
better than shouting at a crowd
huddled in a cold, heavy downpour,
waiting to clamber up out
of the trenches and charge forward
into bullets and be shot dead.
You could have made them scones instead.
What were you thinking?
You were thinking
that death is better than scones,
screaming better than butter.

All my life I've been dogged
by good luck, except
for the bad luck of being born.
Maybe luck itself was lucky enough
never to have been born
except in the human mind,
where it keeps going and going
without even existing,
like the gods that hound us
with barking and howling,
our best friends.

A bottle of champagne
doesn't appear on your lawn
every day, but one did today,
standing upright, silent
in the air swirling with snow.
It came from a poem
by William Carlos Williams
that does not exist
and flew through space and time
to land here, softly,
on my lawn
with no message inside.
Just bubbles.

Humans are barred from bug consciousness.
Worse things have happened,
better ones, too.
Bug climbs up windowpane,
turns right.

Dark and glistening
the shingles on the roof are,
and are happy
as you are happy
to watch the rain
run down them
the way it runs down
the back of your neck
and tells your back
it's alive
as you jump over the house.

I don't think that cherry
is as red as it should be,
in fact it's jet-black,
like paint in a Manet,
but as delicious as a cherry
that is deep red
and ready to float out
into your hands.
That's what happens
when you love art enough
and just stand there
long enough to become an imbecile.

Music is not a tree
nor a cloud nor a punch
in the nose nor
is anything anything else.
Things are just themselves,
isolated in the universe
until we put them together
and pretend they look good
that way, which they do,
actually, and then they drift
into music that's a tree
or a cloud or a punch,
and it doesn't matter which.

It would be funny and creepy
if they found me like this,
feet propped up on the desk,
notebook resting on thighs,
chuff of my hand resting on the page,
pen in right hand.
That's what just happened,
sans them.

When you drop something on the floor
that's the same color as the floor,
it's as if it fell through the floor
because it isn't there anymore.
You look and look, and then
it's there, over there.
You reach down to pick it up
and stop. Maybe
it should stay there,
on its way to another universe,
like the big carrot with human arms and legs
in a drawing by Glen Baxter,
riding an artillery shell
up into the night sky.

7 x 5 x 2 inches = 70 cubic inches,
The Concise Oxford Dictionary,
1,552 pages of astonishment,
until your mind shatters
into a million pieces,
you who at fourteen
read *30 Days to a More Powerful Vocabulary*
and thought it was a snap,
this language. A snap
of the fingers and here you are,
63 years later, holding 70 cubic inches
that hold you in their embrace.

I just took out a ruler
and measured the dictionary
that I had guessed
was 7 x 5 x 2 inches
and guess what?
It was.
I banged the ruler
on the desk and called out
"Yes! Yes! Yes!"
Ah, the small, sad pleasure
of being right.

I leaf through the dictionary
while music comes in
through my ears,
it's Rameau
or someone who sounds like Rameau
as it flows among the words,
notes and letters touching
and becoming each other,
like subatomic particles
that like to fool around
behind what we call our heads.

In early spring
the dead leaves skittered across the lawn
like chipmunks
and then not—
they came back from being chipmunks.
The chipmunks they were
have gone on ahead to the days to come.

When my granddaughter saw me today
a smile lit up her face
and my face opened up too
with a smile that said
I love you and she knew.
Then we looked away
and became
slightly somebody else.

I have come here
to address you
as if
you were an envelope
to be mailed
to a total stranger
who is delighted
to receive anything
but who never thinks
of writing back
to thank you, so
you'll never know
what happened,
just like the other moments
in your life
that go away
bearing a pretty stamp.

I keep trying to have a crush
on every attractive woman I see,
but all I can do
is remember what a crush was
and how it felt
being wagged around by it,
if only a moment or two.
It was fun, that motion,
unlike love, which is not fun.
It can tear your head off.

If only my hand and the pen it holds
could go off on their own
and write what it's like
to be a hand and a pen
attached to the arm of a man
and then to be free of him,
more beautiful and alive
than he could be in his wildest dreams.

I tune in the music station
but when I walk away
it goes buzzy again,
like in the uncertainty principle.
Do you know what that is?
It's a wonderful thing.
It says you can't measure anything accurately
because the act of measuring something
changes it. Or
something like that. Like when
you start to think about eternity
it moves away from you
just beyond your grasp, which
is a major accomplishment for something
so big it can't be measured.

There is nothing like
a house seen from outside,
lights on,
in the dark winter night,
to make you feel
close to all the humans
inside that house
and out.
Pretty great
to love humanity,
if only for a moment.

Five is a nice odd number.
Ask your hand.
Five is also a nice round number,
because the round numbers
are in general so agreeable
they let an odd one stray in
anytime it wanders along,
looking for company
in the lonely world of numbers.
"Okay if I come in?" it asks
and they say, "Sure,
make yourself comfortable
between four and six."
Five would rather sit next to twenty-two,
but figures he'd better not push it.

What a big thing it is
to have a pandemic
that has driven me
into rustic isolation,
where all of nature
is able to kill me
at any time but doesn't,
as if it had forgotten me
in its happy delirium
known as springtime,
of which I form no part,
an innocent bystander
watching the world go crashing by.

A blue hen and a yellow egg
appeared on the piece of paper
and disappeared.
Where did they come from
and where go?
Why do I have to ask?
I should just be glad
they came to see me,
in beautiful blue and yellow.

Last week there was one wasp
in this room, yesterday two,
today five. In a month
there'll be enough of them
to pick me up and throw me
against the wall, but apparently
they don't care about me,
and honestly
I don't care about them either.

I really and truly
would like to let go
of all the low feelings
I've ever had,
to let whatever
else flow in
to take their place,
like helium
in a blimp
at the edge
of sparks,
but I don't think
I could stand
being a blimp.

Oh ho!
More snow

from Norway
I'd say

Let it fall
over all

Norway there
Norway here

At the bottom of a recessed circle
in a small rectangle of wood
are the words
                              The Diabolical Tubes
                              Directions.
                    Slide the Tubes inside each
                       other, so that they appear
                          as one. Then separate
                                them again.
On the other side of the wood is a list
that includes Bear Pit, Mystic Four,
Bunnies, Brahma, Mayblox, the 26,
Multum in Parvo, Chinese, and Peek-a-boo.
At this time
I have no further information
on the Diabolical Tubes.

Like Russell in
the 1974 film
The Dion Brothers
(sometimes *The Gravy Train*)
you feel like shouting—
as he did when he gleefully faced
a danger that would make
most men run like hell—
a rip-roaring "Romp *and* stomp!"
I don't think I've ever heard
three more beautiful words in my life,
or funnier.

My eyes rotate
toward the window
to look outside,
but the curtain is drawn—
all I see is a curtain.
Beyond is snow,
which I'd like to look at
for a moment or so,
but not enough
to make me get up
and pull back the curtain.
I've gotten to where
I'd rather *write about*
pulling back the curtain
and think about italics.
Che piacere strano.

I took a walk through the Bible
and came to a place called the Garden of Eden,
which looked very beautiful,
a nice place to visit
but I wouldn't want to live there.
I prefer jumping through hoops
with lions behind me
trying to bite my ass off.

On a prescription pad
William Carlos Williams
scribbled some notes about poetry,
a few words on each sheet,
some indecipherable.
It looks terrific his scrawl
but it makes you wonder
why he didn't use a regular notebook,
as his mind didn't fit
onto those small sheets.
His mind just jumped into *my* notebook,
which has plenty of room for him.

Used to be when a box
arrived I'd open it right up,
but now I let it sit
for a day or two,
allowing its contents time
to get excited about coming out
and giving me a big Hello.

This year has the nerve
to call itself 2021.
Nothing should be allowed
to call itself 2021.
It's January,
not too late
to turn things around
and get back on track,
like the train you missed
on its way to nowhere
as you banged on its door.

That piece of wood
is scrap lumber.
It has dimensions,
grain, hardness,
and a color
(oldwood color).
No moving parts.
It's just there,
waiting for someone.

My pen wants to bore a hole
through the paper down
into the desk top
to hide itself
from itself.
As they said about the stupid guy:
"He can't chew gum
and chew gum at the same time."

I would like to build a house
based on an exceptionally long sentence
from Marcel Proust or Henry James,
the structure going on and on
to the point where you exclaim
"There's yet *another* room?"
There's always another room,
we just don't know where the door is,
because it's not a noun, it's a conjunction
that, when you turn to look, jumps behind itself.

A single flower
is not half as beautiful
as two flowers,
and six flowers
are not more beautiful
than five.
And then
a clump of yellow daffodils.

There has to be something
I can tell you that
will make you happy
with the idea of being alive,
O citizens. I feel it
somewhere in my body,
where I don't know.
If only my body could disappear,
that one thing
would drop onto the ground,
where you could pick it up
and stare at its words
written in a language
no one understands
but which brings joy,
a quiet, crazy joy without end.

There aren't many more pages in this notebook.
I'll be sorry when they run out,
when they run out of emptiness.

There can't be many more years to my life.
Boo hoo.

I'll go on to a new notebook,
hopefully one without metaphors.

Don't get me wrong.
I like metaphors,
quite a lot.

In fact I live in one.

A book.

DANTE ALIGHIERI THE NEW LIFE
Translated by Dante Gabriel Rossetti; Preface by Michael Palmer

KINGSLEY AMIS COLLECTED POEMS: 1944–1979

YURI ANDRUKHOVYCH SET CHANGE
Translated by Ostap Kin and John Hennessy

ANTONELLA ANEDDA HISTORIAE
Translated by Patrizio Ceccagnoli and Susan Stewart

GUILLAUME APOLLINAIRE ZONE: SELECTED POEMS
Translated by Ron Padgett

AUSTERITY MEASURES THE NEW GREEK POETRY
Edited by Karen Van Dyck

CHARLES BAUDELAIRE FLOWERS OF EVIL
Translated by George Dillon and Edna St. Vincent Millay

SZILÁRD BORBÉLY BERLIN-HAMLET
Translated by Ottilie Mulzet

SZILÁRD BORBÉLY IN A BUCOLIC LAND
Translated by Ottilie Mulzet

ANDRÉ BRETON AND PHILIPPE SOUPAULT THE MAGNETIC
FIELDS
Translated by Charlotte Mandel

MARGARET CAVENDISH *Edited by Michael Robbins*

PAUL CELAN LETTERS TO GISÈLE
Translated by Jason Kavett

AMIT CHAUDHURI Sweet Shop: New and Selected Poems, 1985–202